ENERGIZE YOUR FINGERS EVERY DAY®

Helen Marlais with Timothy Brown

| DAY ONE 1 | DAY TWO 2 | DAY THREE 3 | DAY FOUR 4 | DAY FIVE 5 | DAY SIX 6 |

★ L E S S O N   D A Y

THE
F·J·H
MUSIC
COMPANY
I N C.
Frank J. Hackinson

Production: Frank J. Hackinson
Production Coordinators: Peggy Gallagher and Philip Groeber
Cover: Terpstra Design, San Francisco
Cover and Interior Illustrations: Nina Victor Crittenden, Minneapolis, Minnesota
Text Design and Layout: Terpstra Design, Maritza Cosano Gomez, and Andi Whitmer
Engraving: Tempo Music Press, Inc.
Printer: Tempo Music Press, Inc.

ISBN-13: 978-1-61928-019-9

ABOUT THE AUTHORS

Dr. Marlais is one of the most prolific authors in the field of educational piano music and an exclusive writer for The FJH Music Company Inc. The critically acclaimed and award-winning piano series: *Succeeding at the Piano®–A Method for Everyone, Succeeding with the Masters®, The Festival Collection®, In Recital®, Sight Reading and Rhythm Every Day®, Write, Play, and Hear Your Theory Every Day®,* and *The FJH Contemporary Keyboard Editions,* among others, included in *The FJH Pianist's Curriculum®* by Helen Marlais, are designed to guide students from the beginner through advanced levels. Dr. Marlais gives pedagogical workshops worldwide and the method *Succeeding at the Piano®* is published in South Korea and Taiwan. She presents showcases for The FJH Music Company at national conventions and internationally.

Dr. Marlais has performed and presented throughout the U.S. and in Canada, Italy, England, France, Hungary, Turkey, Germany, Lithuania, Estonia, Australia, New Zealand, China, South Korea, Taiwan, and Russia. She has recorded on Gasparo, Centaur and Audite record labels with her husband, concert clarinetist Arthur Campbell. Their recording, *Music for Clarinet and Piano,* was nominated for the 2013 *International Classical Music Awards,* one of the most prestigious distinctions available to classical musicians today. She has also recorded numerous educational piano CD's for Stargrass Records®. She has performed with members of the Chicago, Pittsburgh, Minnesota, Grand Rapids, Des Moines, Cedar Rapids, and Beijing National Symphony Orchestras, and has premiered many new works by contemporary composers from the United States, Canada, and Europe.

Dr. Marlais received her DM in piano performance and pedagogy from Northwestern University, her MFA in piano performance from Carnegie Mellon University, and was awarded the Outstanding Alumna in the Arts from the University of Toledo, where she received her bachelor of music degree in piano performance. As well as being the Director of Keyboard Publications for The FJH Music Company, Dr. Marlais is also an Associate Professor of Music at Grand Valley State University in Grand Rapids, Michigan. Visit: www.helenmarlais.com

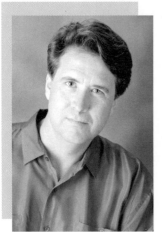

Timothy Brown's music has been influenced greatly by the Italian film composer Ennio Morricone. His music is noted for its "immediate emotional impact" and its roots in the neo-romantic style of music composition. Traditional formal structural elements are embedded in his wide array of compositions which includes orchestral, ballet, choral and chamber works and a body of work specifically written for piano and pedagogical purposes. He did his undergraduate studies at Bowling Green State University and received his master's degree in piano performance from the University of North Texas. His past teachers include Adam Wodnicki, Newel Kay Brown and Robert Xavier Rodriguez. He was a recipient of a research fellowship from Royal Holloway, University of London, where he performed his postgraduate studies in music composition and orchestration with the English composer, Brian Lock. He later continued his research at the well-known Accademia Nazionale di Santa Cecilia in Rome, Italy.

His numerous credits as a composer include the first prize at the Aliénor International Harpsichord Competition for his harpsichord solo *Suite Española* (Centaur records). His works are frequently performed throughout North America and Europe, and at numerous international venues including The World Piano Pedagogy Conference, and the Festival Internacional de Música de Tecla Española in the Andalusian town of Almeria, Spain. His music has been performed by concert artists, Helen Marlais, Elaine Funaro, and Arthur Campbell. Recent programs include his original compositions showcased at the Spoleto Music Festival, and the Library of Congress Concert Series in Washington D.C.

His recent commissions and performances include world premieres by the Chapman University Chamber Orchestra and Concert Choir, the Carter Albrecht Music Foundation, the Rodgers Center for Holocaust Education, and the Daniel Pearl Music Foundation, and a commissioned work and article by the American composer, Denes Agay, for Clavier Magazine. Recent works also include a commissioned Ballet by the Dallas Ballet Foundation to write the orchestral score for the Ballet Petite, *The Happy Prince* based on a short story by Oscar Wilde. Timothy Brown is an exclusive composer/clinician for The FJH Music Company Inc.

TABLE OF CONTENTS

Unit 1

In this book, you will practice eight techniques. Once they become a habit, you will play with beauty, speed, and ease!

1) **Good Posture:**

Playing with good posture is the Number 1 way to play with a healthy, tension-free body and create an excellent sound.

Imagine a basketball player. What would happen if he/she tried to make baskets while having a slouched back? He/she wouldn't be able to make too many baskets! The same is true for pianists—sit tall at the bench, letting your spine lengthen and let your head float on top of a tension-free neck.

Then, lean slightly forward into the keyboard with your upper torso, so that you can play with power and confidence.

2) **Arm Weight:**

Don't wait to use arm weight! Practice dropping your forearm and wrist at the same time to the bottom of the key for a great sound. The opposite approach, which is not correct, is to play with stiff wrists, playing only on the top of the keys.

Imagine a downhill skier who was told not to move his/her knees up and down naturally when skiing down a mountain. He/she wouldn't be able to go very far! The same is true for pianists—let your wrists and forearms drop naturally to the bottom of the key, and then release by rolling your wrist slightly forward. This will result in a beautiful sound and feel.

Good   **Not Good**

FJH2165

3) Flexible Wrists:

Playing with flexible wrists will help you play with easy motions, as well as help you to make beautiful musical sounds.

How to do it:

a) Rest fingers 2 and 3 gently on your thigh or on a tabletop.

b) Roll your left wrist in a clockwise motion.

c) Next, roll your right wrist in a counter-clockwise motion.

d) Notice that the hand, forearm, and elbow move along with the wrist.

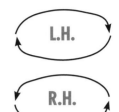

When you use arm weight, along with flexible wrists, you will be able to play tension-free, which is very important.

Imagine a runner who always ran without moving his/her ankles! The runner wouldn't be able to go very far or fast! The same is true for pianists—let your arms and wrists move naturally so that you play with well-coordinated motion.

4) Strong Fingers:

Playing with strong fingers will help you play evenly and with a beautiful tone. It is important to play with strong fingers that do not "dent" in at the first knuckle joint.

Imagine a ballet dancer who tried to dance on point with her ankles moving this way and that! The dancer wouldn't be able to stay upright! The same is true for pianists—let your fingers be strong so that you can play well!

How to do it:

a) Solidly tap your 2nd finger on a table top or on the closed lid of the piano. Keep the weight of the forearm centered over the finger that is playing. Focus on how the cushion of your finger pad makes contact with the table top/lid. Keep your wrist level with your forearm.

b) Tap by moving from the top knuckle that forms the strong bridge of your hand.

c) Now tap with the 3rd, then 4th, then 5th fingers in the same way. Don't *press* into the keys. This causes tension.

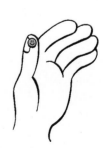

d) When tapping with your thumb, keep in mind to play on the **outside tip** of your thumbnail. Playing on the full, flat side of your thumb collapses the wrists and causes tension in your fingers and underneath your wrist.

5) Free Arm:

Using a free arm will allow you to play with control, ease, and agility. Keep in mind that when playing, your fingers, hands, wrists, and arms should **move together**, at the same time, as **one playing unit**.

Imagine a strong bridge from your shoulder to your fingertips. When you play, feel that your forearm supports each finger by having it directly behind and centered over each finger in use.

Learning to shift your weight from one finger to the next will also help you play with a beautiful sound. You will be able to play fast passages quickly and evenly, and slow passages with great control. It will help you to *not* play with stiff wrists!

Imagine a surfer who tried to surf with his/her legs moving this way and that as well as their arms moving this way and that! The surfer wouldn't be able to stay up on his/her surfboard! The same is true for pianists—let your arms, wrists, and fingers move together at the same time so your playing is effortless and the sound is beautiful and your motions are fluid and easy.

Remind yourself to notice your upper arm moving freely when you play.

6) Two-note slurs:

A mark of a fine musician is one who plays expressively. Playing two-note slurs well helps you play musically.

Imagine a diver diving into the water and then lifting himself to the top of the water. The same is true for pianists—drop your wrist with arm weight on the first note of each two-note slur. Then play the second note with a quieter sound. While you play the second key, roll your hand forward onto your fingertip and then lift, wrist first.

FJH2165

7) Rotation:

This important technique helps you move from one key to another without stretching or reaching. Use a free arm in this technique to move freely from one finger to the next.

Imagine that your forearms, wrists, and hands rock from side to side, the same way a boat rocks gently from side to side when it is docked in water.

The fingers, hand, wrist, and forearm **move together**, at the same time, side to side. The elbow stays loose at your side.

Play on the outside tip of your thumb nail.

Imagine an obstacle course where an athlete has to run on either side of a stream—left foot, then right foot, left foot, then right foot. The athlete will need to throw his/her weight from side to side so that they don't land in the water! The same approach works for this rotation technique.

How to do it:
a) Prepare your fingers over the keys.

b) Rotate your hand, wrist, and arm in the direction of the next finger that plays. Keep your wrist in line with your forearm and hand.

c) The rotation gesture will be small if the interval is small, and larger if the interval is larger.

8) Balance Between the Hands:

Listening to and bringing out the hand that has the melody makes you a fine musician!

Imagine a rowing team rowing a boat in a competition. The rowing team in the boat is like a melody in music, and the water underneath them is like the harmony in music.

1

A Balanced Body Plays the Piano Well: Remember Your Healthy Posture!

- Notice your head balanced on top of your neck.
- Sit tall and long.

Walking and Jogging
(arm weight, free arm)

2

Jumping Over Rocks
(free arm, strong fingers)

DID IT!

8

Outer Space Conversation
(free arm, flexible wrists)

Look Who's Right Behind!
(five-finger patterns, strong fingers)

* Play with strong fingers that do not dent at the first knuckle joint.

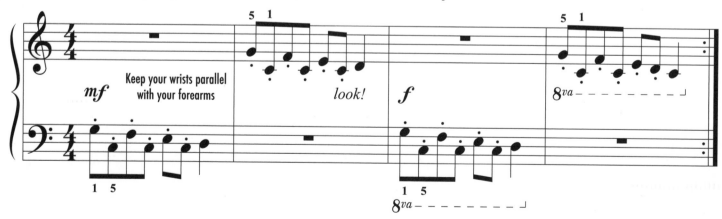

DID IT!

FJH2165

Horses Trotting
(flexible wrists, strong fingers)

mf Push off each triad, wrist first

Check for no dents!

Mr. Jack Rabbit
(free arm, rotation)

f legato

Increase the tempo everyday, always playing evenly!

DID IT!

★ LESSON DAY

• Play your favorite piece of the week for your teacher. Then, your teacher may have you play another one.

Teacher comments: _____

Unit 3

Sitting on the Bench
The Right Height and Distance

- Sit comfortably on the piano bench.
- Move your arms in—to the middle of the black keys—as if playing.
- Can you easily swing your elbows from side to side?
- Are your elbows slightly above the top of the white keys?
  Sitting at the right height and distance from the keyboard will
  make piano playing easier.

Walking on a Tightrope
(two-note slurs)

Play with your L.H. one octave lower.

DID IT!

Dropping a Rock in a Well
(free arm, broken triads)

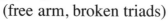

DID IT!

3
DAY THREE

A Boat on the Water
(balance between the hands)

Bring out the melody.
Play the L.H. silently, then play it quietly.

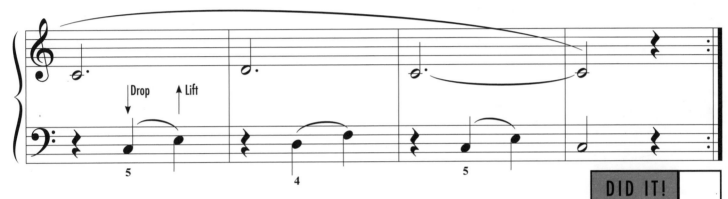

Drop   Lift

DID IT!

4
DAY FOUR

A Big Fish Under the Water
(balance between the hands)

Drop   Roll forward and then lift

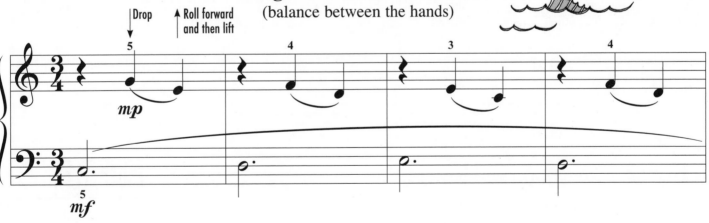

DID IT!

Running a Race
(strong fingers, flexible wrists)

* Play with strong fingers that do not dent at the first knuckle joint.

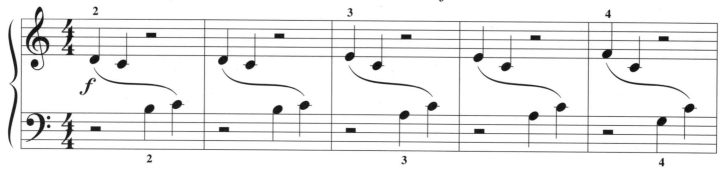

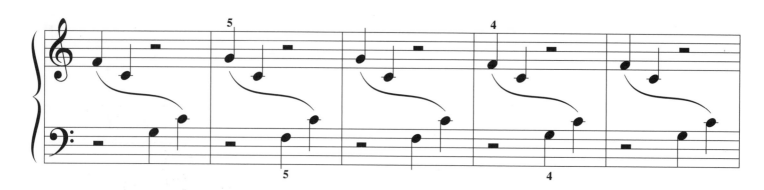

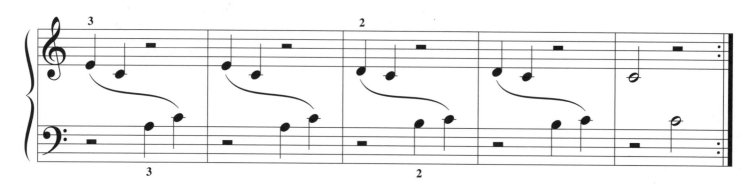

Increase the tempo everyday, always playing evenly!

DID IT!

Pulling Tissue From a Box
(three-note slurs)

Marching Confidently
(arm weight)

DID IT!

• Play your favorite piece of the week for your teacher. Then, your teacher may have you play another one.

Teacher comments: _____

Unit 4

1
DAY ONE

Release the Muscles in Your Neck!

- Move your neck up, down, to the right, and to the left.
- Now slowly move it all around.
- This will help you play without tension in your neck.

Gecko on the Wall
(strong fingers, flexible wrists)

*Look for the shape of a letter "C" between your second finger and thumb.

mf legato

Play with the R.H. two octaves higher

DID IT!

2
DAY TWO

Lost, then Found
(strong fingers)

f legato

DID IT!

16

FJH2165

Bounding Through a Meadow
(five-finger patterns, free arm, flexible wrists)

mf Roll wrists over, around, and to the left. Stay close to the keys.

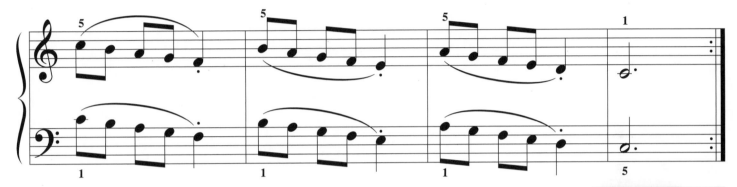

DID IT!

Doing Push-Ups
(free arm, arm weight)

*Drop your arm weight on every key. Play on your finger pads.

f legato

DID IT!

Baby Bear Walking in the Raindrops
(balance between the hands)

Mamma Bear Walking in the Raindrops
(balance between the hands)

DID IT!

FJH2165

Riding Piggyback
(free arm, rotation)

An Airplane Above the Clouds
(balance between the hands)

DID IT!

★ LESSON DAY

• Play your favorite piece of the week for your teacher. Then, your teacher may have you play another one.

Teacher comments: _____

FJH2165

19

1

Relax Your Shoulders

- Move your right shoulder up, then down.
- Move your left shoulder up, then down.
- Then roll your shoulders back, and then swing them in.
- Now release your shoulders and keep them low and wide.

Little Boy Dancing
(five-finger patterns, rotation)

▲ Roll your wrist forward and push out of the key

Now transpose to CM.

DID IT!

2

Little Girl Dancing
(five-finger patterns, rotation)

▲ Push forward and out of the key

Now transpose to CM.

No Dent!

Dog Chasing its Tail
(rotation)

* Keep your "Perfect Piano Hand" shape!

Now transpose to GM.

DID IT!

Dutch Clog Dance
(two-note slurs)

Now transpose to DM.

DID IT!

Swinging Side to Side
(free arm, rotation)

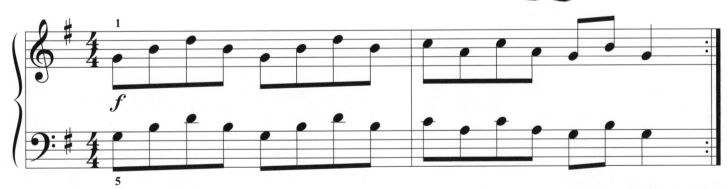

Now transpose to DM.

DID IT!

Leaping in Ballet Class
(arm weight, free arm)

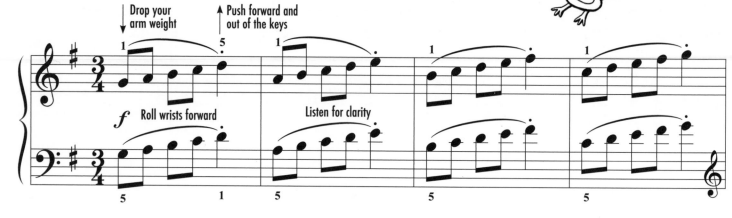

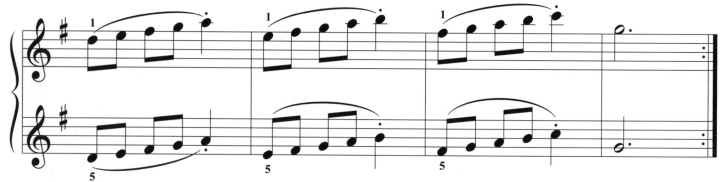

Pillow Fight!
(arm weight, strong fingers)

* Lift your wrists slightly to prepare for each drop. After dropping into the keys, look for no dents!
Then lift your wrists and forearms together, at the same time.

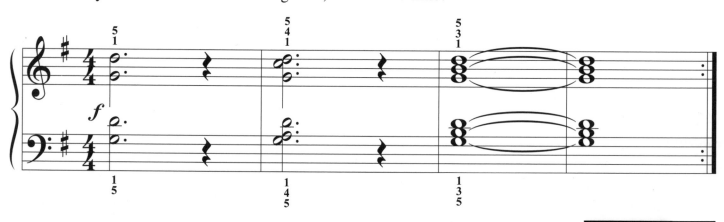

DID IT!

Skating on Ice
(balance between the hands, flexible wrists)

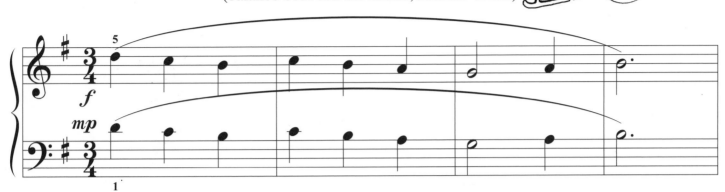

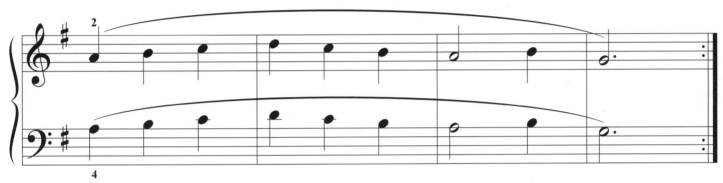

Now transpose to other keys.

Hot Potatoes!
(strong fingers)

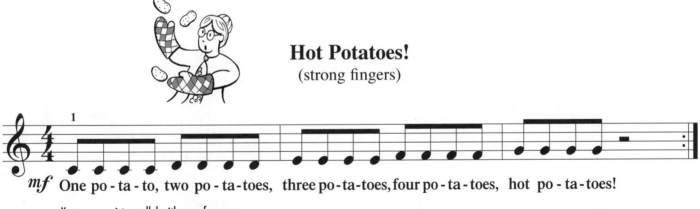

mf One po - ta - to, two po - ta - toes, three po - ta - toes, four po - ta - toes, hot po - ta - toes!

Keep your wrist parallel with your forearm

Now try it with your L.H. | DID IT!

★ LESSON DAY

• Play your favorite piece of the week for your teacher. Then, your teacher may have you play another one.

Teacher comments: _____

Unit 6

1

DAY ONE

Excellent Posture Feels Good

- Sit quietly on the piano bench with your hands comfortably on your thighs.
- Breathe in slowly . . . 1 . . . 2 . . . 3 . . . feel your stomach grow as you breathe in.
- Exhale slowly . . . 1 . . . 2 . . . 3 . . . notice how your stomach goes back to normal.

The Moose and the Squirrel
(free arm, three-note slurs)

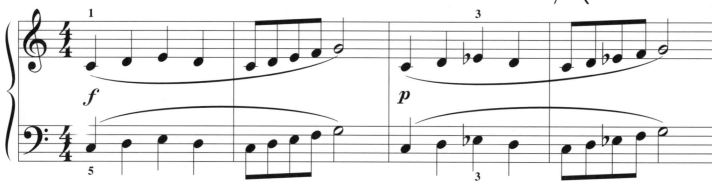

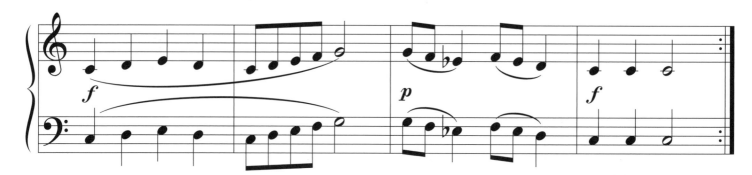

DID IT! ☐

2

DAY TWO

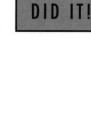

High Speed Train
(rotation)

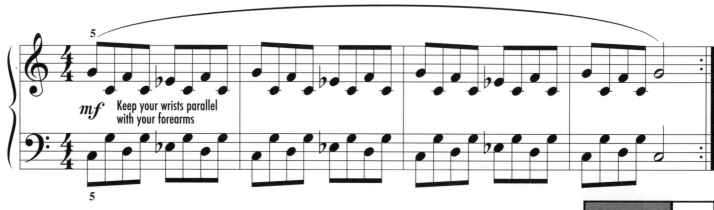

DID IT! ☐

24

FJH2165

Tapping My Head with My L.H. at the Same Time I Rub My Belly with My R.H.

(balance between the hands)

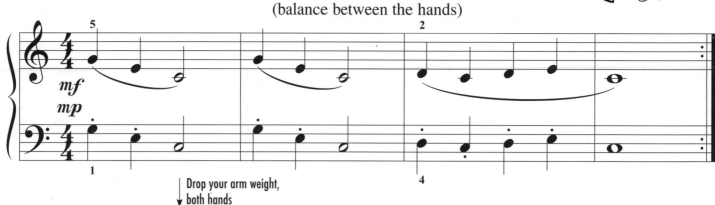

Drop your arm weight, both hands

Tapping My Head with My R.H. at the Same Time I Rub My Belly with My L.H.

(flexible wrists, arm weight)

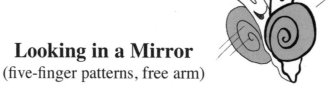

Looking in a Mirror

(five-finger patterns, free arm)

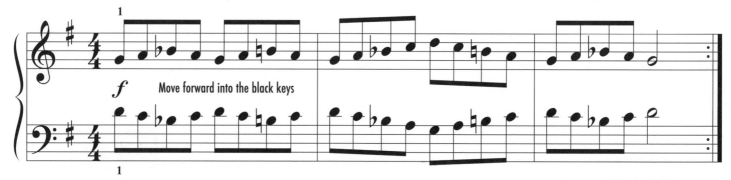

Move forward into the black keys

Now transpose to other keys.

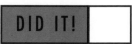

DID IT!

Increase the tempo everyday, always playing evenly!

FJH2165

Roller Coaster Ride
(strong fingers)

* Keep your wrists parallel with your forearms.

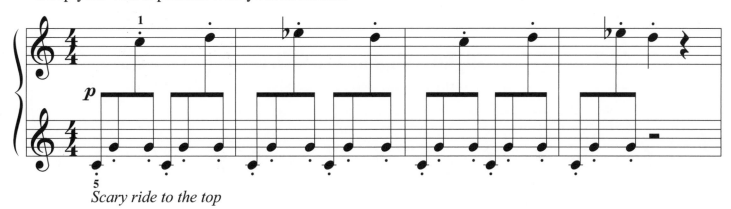

Scary ride to the top

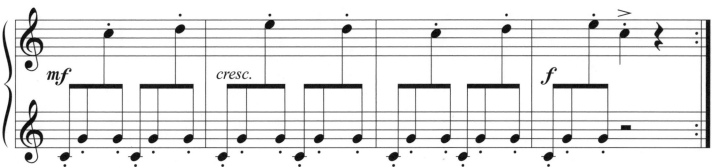

Much more fun coming down

Two Birds Chattering
(three-note slurs, flexible wrists)

DID IT!

★ LESSON DAY

• Play your favorite piece of the week for your teacher. Then, your teacher may have you play another one.

Teacher comments: _____

Unit 7

Good Posture—Getting Ready to Play!

- Sit toward the front half of the bench with your body weight evenly distributed between your feet and the seat.
- Lean your upper body in toward the piano, letting your center of gravity be over the keys you play.

Slightly Mad at My Sister
(arm weight, strong fingers)

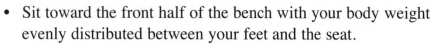

mf Keep your wrists parallel with your forearms

Drop arm weight

DID IT!

Dragonflies
(strong fingers)

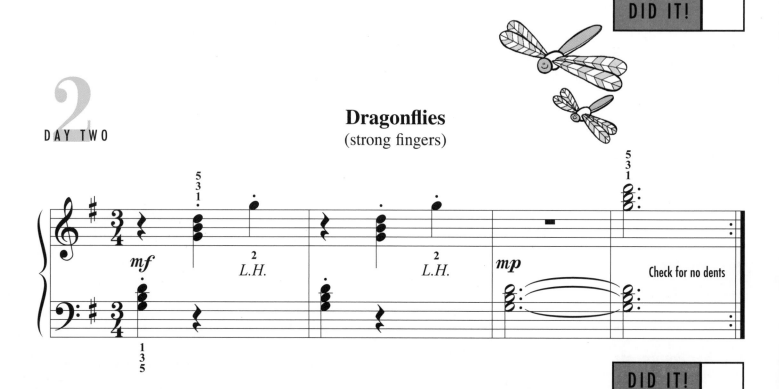

mf   2 *L.H.*   2 *L.H.*   *mp*   Check for no dents

DID IT!

FJH2165

3

DAY THREE

A Seal with a Ball

(broken and blocked triads, flexible wrists)

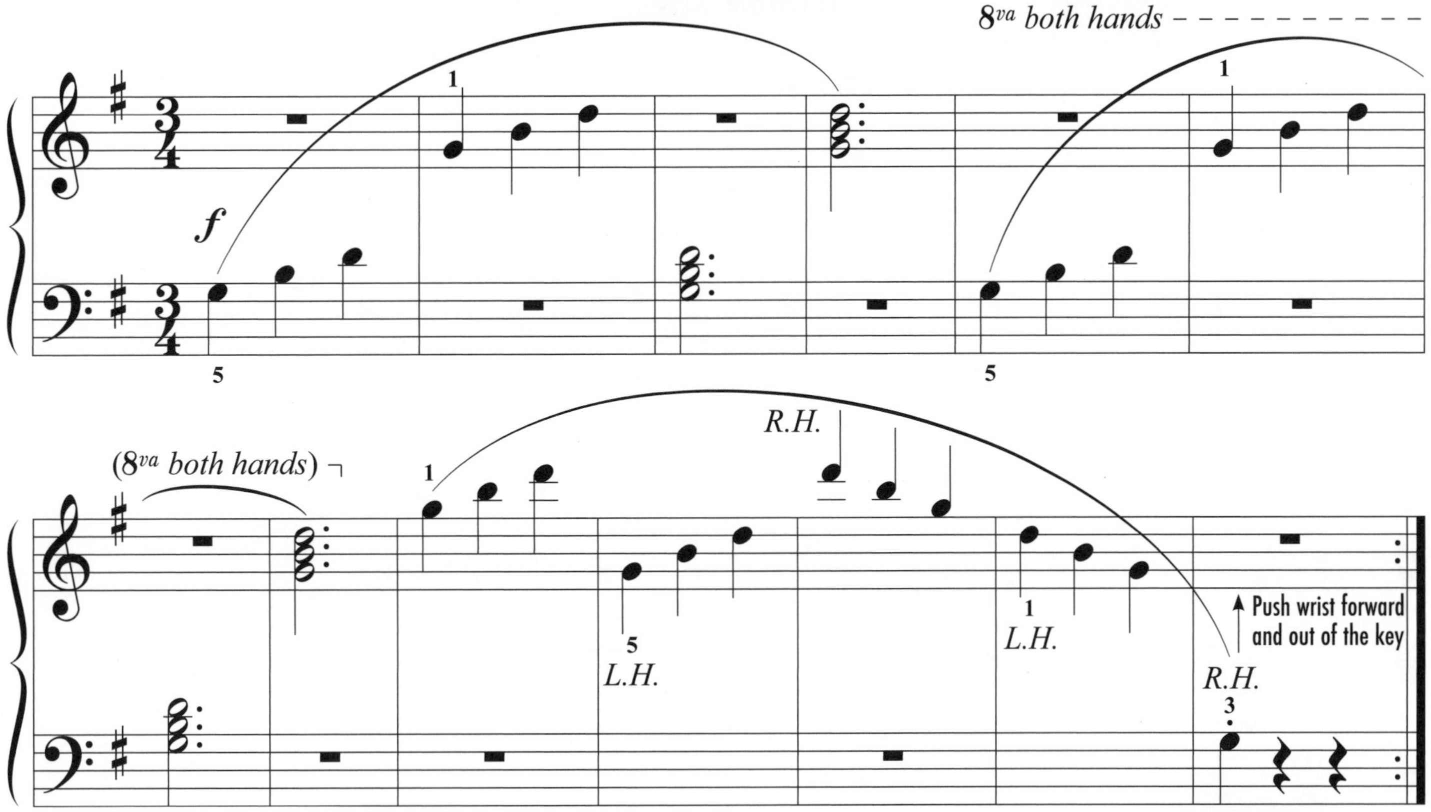

DID IT!

4

DAY FOUR

Confident and Brave!

(strong fingers)

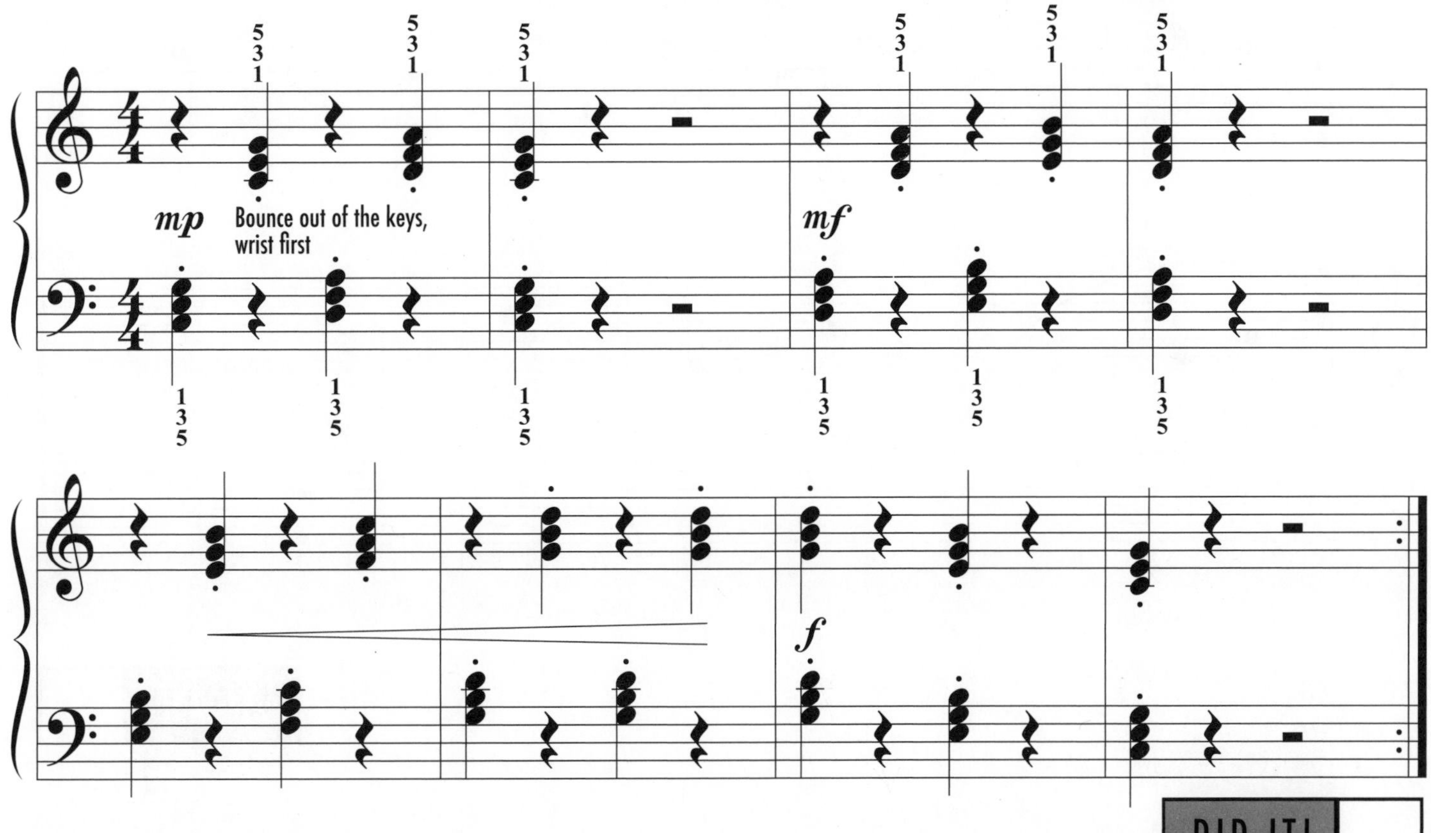

DID IT!

Water Droplets on the Lake
(flexible wrists)

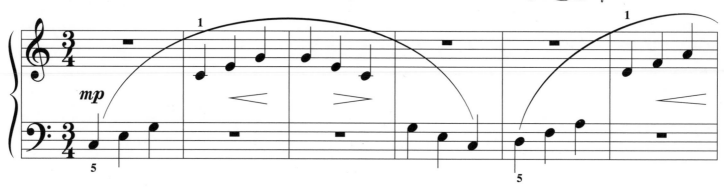

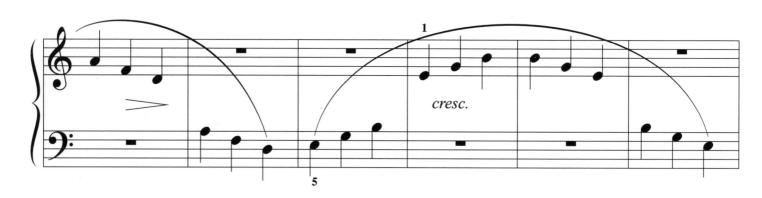

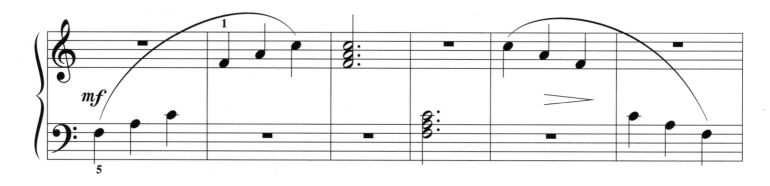

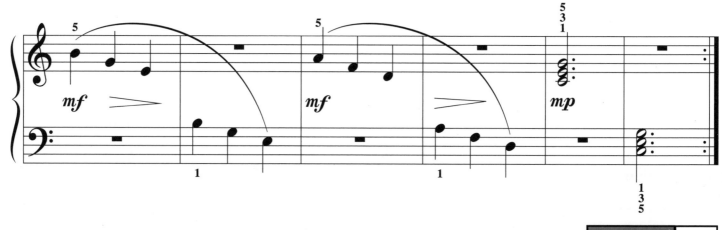

DID IT!

FJH2165

Raising the Flag
(arm weight, flexible wrists)

Drop arm weight

Lift slowly out of the keys

8va both hands

A Boy on Tip-Toe
(strong fingers)

mf See the boy, on tip-toe, see the boy, on tip-toe, see the boy, on tip-toe!

Keep your wrist parallel with your forearm

Increase the tempo everyday always playing evenly! Now try it with your L.H.

DID IT!

★ LESSON DAY

• Play your favorite piece of the week for your teacher. Then, your teacher may have you play another one.

Teacher comments: _____

Unit 8

Making a Healthy Body for Playing

- Stand tall. Move your arms through the air and up to the sky.
  Imagine you are making angel's wings.
- Then move your arms down to your sides.
- Do this four times slowly.

Playing Chess
(balance between the hands)

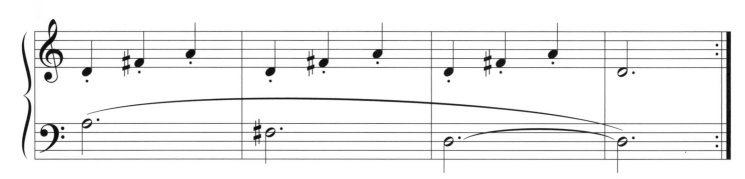

DID IT!

Dancing Mice
(three-note slurs)

DID IT!

FJH2165

Slightly Mad at My Brother
(arm weight, rotation)

mf

cresc.

f

DID IT!

Cross-Country Skiing
(rotation)

mf

f

Now transpose to other keys.

DID IT!

Copy Cat
(three-note slurs, flexible wrists)

Playing Hockey
(free arm, strong fingers)

Now transpose to E Major.

DID IT!

Playing Ping-Pong
(arm weight)

* Keep your wrists parallel with your forearms.

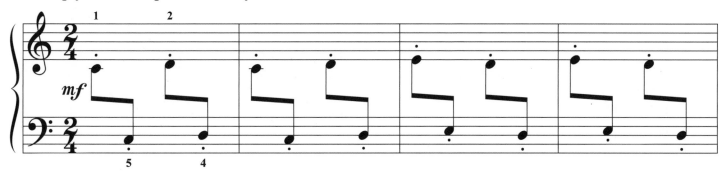

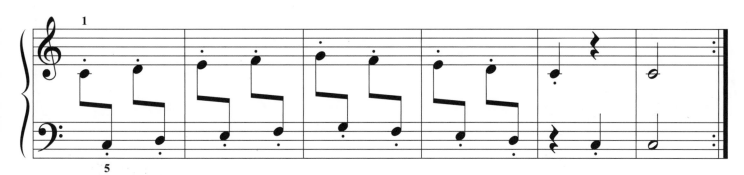

Now transpose to DM.

Doing the Hula-Hoop
(balance between the hands)

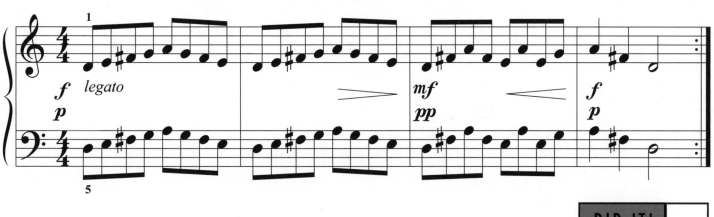

DID IT! ☐

⭐ LESSON DAY

• Play your favorite piece of the week for your teacher. Then, your teacher may have you play another one.

Teacher comments: _____

Unit 9

DAY ONE

Release the Tension in Your Arms

- Move your hands, wrists, arms and elbows forward,
  away from your body.
- Then move them towards you, then to the left, and to the right.
- Think north, south, west, and east, always moving in a flowing motion.

Tetrachords

T = tonic
W = whole step
W = whole step
H = half step

A scale is made up of two tetrachords.

Up and Down the Ladder

(The C Major Scale using Two Tetrachords)

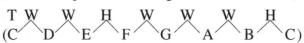

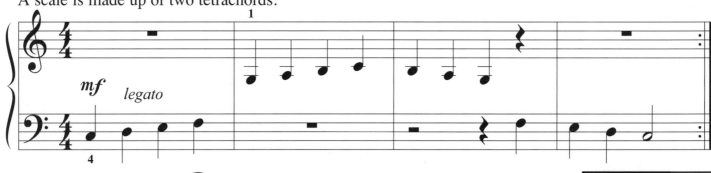

DID IT!

DAY TWO

Up and Down the Stairs

(The G Major Scale using Two Tetrachords)

Up and Down the Hill

(The D Major Scale using Two Tetrachords)

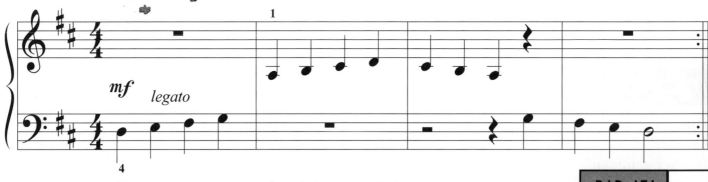

How many other tetrachords can you play? Try every key!

DID IT!

FJH216

DAY THREE

Watching a Tennis Match in the Morning
(crossing left over right hand, strong fingers)

DAY FOUR

Watching a Tennis Match in the Afternoon
(crossing right over left hand, strong fingers)

DID IT!

DID IT!

In a Pirate Ship
(two-note slurs, arm weight)

Check for no dents and "Perfect Piano Hands"

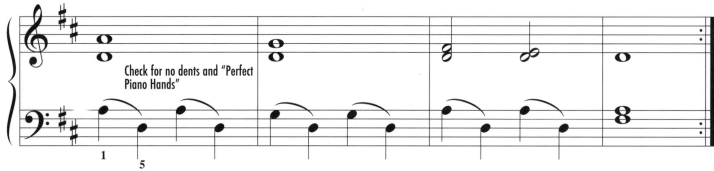

Fixing the Roof
(arm weight)

*Lift your wrists slightly to prepare for each drop. After dropping into the keys, look for no dents! Then lift your wrists and forearms together, at the same time.

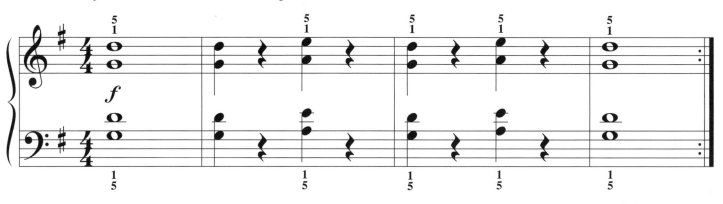

DID IT!

Jumping In and Out of The Waves
(flexible wrists, strong fingers)

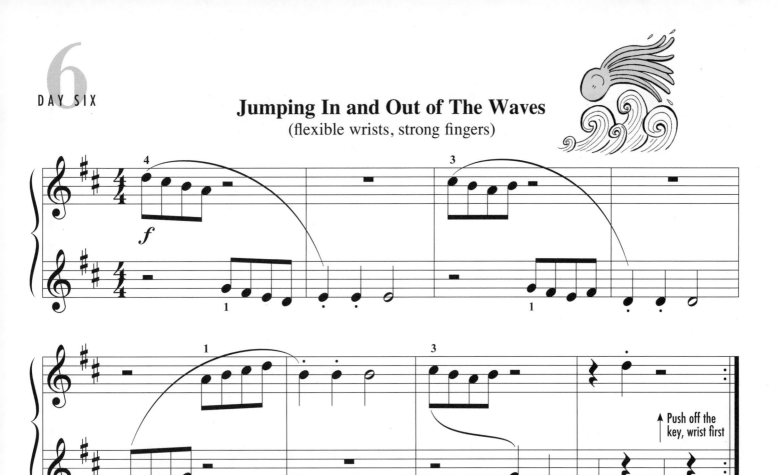

▲ Push off the
key, wrist first

Driving a Sports Car
(rotation)

* Everyday, play this piece faster and faster!

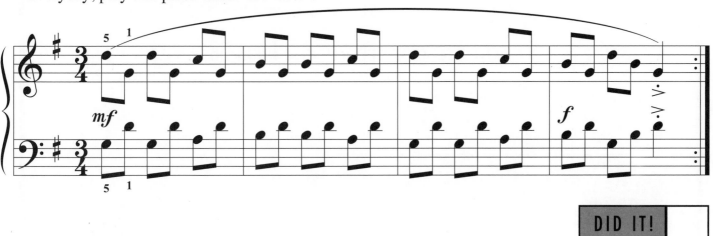

DID IT!

★ LESSON DAY

• Play your favorite piece of the week for your teacher. Then, your teacher may have you play another one.

Teacher comments: _____

Certificate of Achievement

_____

has successfully completed

ENERGIZE YOUR FINGERS EVERY DAY®

BOOK 2A

of The FJH Pianist's Curriculum®

You are now ready for **Book 2B**

_____
Date

_____
Teacher's Signature